LEVEL
1

MARVEL

SPIDER-MAN
BUGS OUT!

Daka Hermon

NATIONAL
GEOGRAPHIC

Washington, D.C.

For Devin, who is super in every way —Daka

Published by National Geographic Partners, LLC, Washington, DC 20036.

Copyright © 2024 National Geographic Partners, LLC

Designed by Gustavo Tello

The author and publisher gratefully acknowledge the literacy review of this book by Mariam Jean Dreher, professor emerita of reading education, University of Maryland, College Park, and expert review by Dr. William Lamp.

Photo Credits
AS= Adobe Stock; MP= Minden Pictures; NPL= Nature Picture Library; SS=Shutterstock

Cover: (CTR), © 2024 MARVEL; (LE), © Jürgen Otto; (UP LE), © 2024 MARVEL; (LO LE), © 2024 MARVEL; (BACKGROUND RT), © 2024 MARVEL; (HEADER THROUGHOUT), © 2024 MARVEL; (BACKGROUND THROUGHOUT), © 2024 MARVEL; 1 (BACKGROUND), © 2024 MARVEL; 1 (CTR), © 2024 MARVEL; 1 (UP CTR), © 2024 MARVEL; 1 (UP LE), Alen Thien/SS; 1 (LO LE), Stephen Dalton/NPL; 1 (CTR RT), Piotr Naskrecki/MP; 3 (UP RT CTR), © 2024 MARVEL; 3 (UP RT), © 2024 MARVEL; 3 (LO), © 2024 MARVEL; 4-5, Lee/AS; 4 (LO LE), Huw Cordey/NPL; 5, © 2024 MARVEL; 6 (UP), The Natural History Museum, London/Science Source; 6 (LO), © 2024 MARVEL; 7 (UP), fotomaster/AS; 7 (LO RT), Kampan/AS; 7 (LO CTR CTR), © 2024 MARVEL; 7 (LO CTR), Kapitosh/SS; 8-9, Pete Oxford/MP; 8 (joke emoji), © 2024 MARVEL; 8 (joke emoji), © 2024 MARVEL; 9 (CTR), © 2024 MARVEL; 9 (webby words icon), © 2024 MARVEL; 10 (UP LE), © 2024 MARVEL; 10 (UP CTR), © 2024 MARVEL; 10-11 (BACKGROUND), Stephen Dalton/NPL; 11 (joke emoji), © 2024 MARVEL; 11 (UP LE), PREMAPHOTOS/NPL; 11 (LO RT), Amani A/AS; 11 (joke emoji), © 2024 MARVEL; 12 (UP LE), Adam Fletcher/Biosphoto; 12 (CTR), Adam Fletcher/Biosphoto/MP; 12 (CTR RT), © 2024 MARVEL; 12 (UP RT), © Jürgen Otto; 13 (joke emoji), © 2024 MARVEL; 13 (joke emoji), © 2024 MARVEL; 13 (UP RT), © 2024 MARVEL; 13 (CTR LE), © Jürgen Otto; 13 (LO RT), © Jürgen Otto; 13 (webby words icon), © 2024 MARVEL; 14 (UP RT), © 2024 MARVEL; 14-15 (BACKGROUND), © 2024 MARVEL; 14 (LO LE), © 2024 MARVEL; 14 (CTR LE), Sam DCruz/SS; 14 (CTR RT), Alcuin/AS; 14 (LO), I Wayan Sumatika/AS; 15 (LO RT), © 2024 MARVEL; 15 (UP), Satoshi Kuribayashi/Nature Production/MP; 15 (CTR), Thierry Berrod, Mona Lisa Production/Science Source; 15 (LO), as_trofey/AS; 16 (CTR LE), © 2024 MARVEL; 16 (CTR RT), Neil Phillips/Alamy Stock Photo; 17 (joke emoji), © 2024 MARVEL; 17 (LO RT), Auscape/Universal Images Group/Getty Images; 17 (joke emoji), © 2024 MARVEL; 17 (webby words icon), © 2024 MARVEL; 18, Chien Lee/MP; 19 (UP), Alen Thien/SS; 19 (RT), © 2024 MARVEL; 20 (LO), frank29052515/AS; 20 (LE), © 2024 MARVEL; 21 (UP), Elkspera/AS; 21 (LO RT), © 2024 MARVEL; 22 (UP LE), © 2024 MARVEL; 22-23, Piotr Naskrecki/MP; 23 (LO RT), © 2024 MARVEL; 23 (joke emoji), © 2024 MARVEL; 23 (emoji), © 2024 MARVEL; 24 (LO), Gerry/AS; 24 (UP), Morley Read/NPL; 25 (LO), Steve Byland/AS; 25 (UP), © 2024 MARVEL; 25 (joke emoji), © 2024 MARVEL; 25 (joke emoji), © 2024 MARVEL; 26-27 (BACKGROUND), Cheattha/AS; 26 (webby words icon), © 2024 MARVEL; 27, © 2024 MARVEL; 28 (UP), © 2024 MARVEL; 28 (LO RT), Huw Cordey/NPL; 28 (LO CTR), © 2024 MARVEL; 29 (BACKGROUND), © 2024 MARVEL; 29 (UP LE), © 2024 MARVEL; 29 (UP RT), © 2024 MARVEL; 29 (LO LE), © 2024 MARVEL; 29 (LO CTR RT), © 2024 MARVEL; 29 (LO RT), © 2024 MARVEL; 29 (CTR), © 2024 MARVEL; 29 (LO CTR LE), © 2024 MARVEL; 30 (LO LE), Aubord Dulac/AS; 30 (LO RT), PREMAPHOTOS/NPL; 30 (CTR RT), © 2024 MARVEL; 31 (UP LE), Jay Ondreicka/SS; 31 (UP RT), constantincornel/AS; 31 (LO LE), OlegD/AS; 31 (LO RT), lazalnik/AS; 32 (UP LE), Pete Oxford/MP; 32 (LO LE), Adam Fletcher/Biosphoto/MP; 32 (CTR RT), frank29052515/AS; 32 (LO RT), ridho/AS; 32 (UP RT), © 2024 MARVEL

Trade paperback ISBN: 978-1-4263-7685-6
Reinforced library binding ISBN: 978-1-4263-7690-0

Printed in the United States of America
24/WOR/1

Contents

Super-Powers

Who can climb high, jump far, and shoot webs? It's your friendly neighborhood Spider-Man ... and a spider!

Darwin's bark spider

What other
bugs have powers
like super heroes? Follow along as
Spider-Man and his friends discover
the super things bugs can do!

Super Strength and Size

What's big and strong like Spider-Man's friend the Hulk? The titan beetle. It's one of the largest beetles in the world.

The
titan beetle
can grow up
to 6.5 inches
(16.5 cm) long. That's
bigger than a hot dog!

Its powerful jaws, called
mandibles, can snap a
pencil in two!

HULK
SMASH!

Hercules beetles are the strongest insects in the world. They can carry up to 80 times their weight. That's like the Hulk holding seven elephants!

Hercules beetles
are herbivores.
These healthy
eaters love fruit.

WEBBY Words

HERBIVORE: An animal
that eats plants

Mighty Jumpers

TAWIP

Ready, set, jump!
Spider-Man uses his
web-shooters to leap
from building to building
in New York City.

Froghoppers are champion jumpers,
too. They use their short legs to send
themselves high into the air.

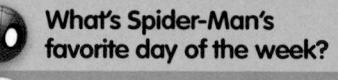

Look at that bubbly foam! It's their protective hideout.

European robin

WATCH OUT! Birds, spiders, and frogs love to eat froghoppers.

A peacock spider is the size of a grain of rice.

Peacock spiders are tiny, but they can jump far—a little more than half a foot (15 cm)—to catch their prey. Gotcha!

 What do super heroes like Spider-Man and Ant-Man have in common?

They bug villains!

They love to dance! Male peacock spiders dance to show off for female peacock spiders.

THIS PEACOCK SPIDER MATCHES MY SUIT!

PREY: An animal that is eaten by another animal

6 Super-Strange BUGGY FACTS

1 A COCKROACH CAN HOLD ITS BREATH FOR 40 MINUTES.

2 HOUSEFLIES CAN WALK BACKWARD AND CLIMB ANY SURFACE, LIKE SPIDER-MAN.

3 CENTIPEDES CAN HEAL THEMSELVES, JUST LIKE WOLVERINE.

4

VENOM IS NO MATCH FOR A BOMBARDIER BEETLE'S BOILING LIQUID SPRAY.

5

THE GIANT WETA, THE WORLD'S HEAVIEST INSECT, HAS BEEN AROUND SINCE THE TIME OF THE DINOSAURS.

6

SCIENTISTS THINK THERE MAY BE 10 QUINTILLION INSECTS (10,000,000,000,000,000,000) ON EARTH!

Super Speed

Quicksilver is the fastest super hero, but he has some bugs to beat!

Dragonflies are one of the speediest flying insects in the world. They can fly up to 35 miles an hour (56 km/h). These insects can fly backward and hover.

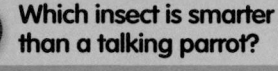
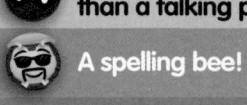
The tiger beetle is the fastest running insect in the world! These teeny predators race to catch other insects at 5.5 miles an hour (9 km/h).

WEBBY Words

PREDATOR: An animal that hunts and eats other animals

Night Vision

Crickets can
see in the dark!
Night vision
helps crickets
find food and
other crickets.

But that's not their only skill. Crickets can make music! They chirp by rubbing their legs on their wings. They could join Gwen Stacy in a band!

Teamwork

Many bugs work together like the Avengers! Ants live in colonies. They use teamwork to dig nests and cross over water.

ANTS WORK TOGETHER LIKE US, WASP!

Bees team up
to build honeycombs
in their hives. Working
together, they find nectar
to make honey.

Body Armor

SPIDEY, THIS BUG'S GOT STYLE!

Some bugs have suits of strong armor like Iron Man.

The ironclad beetle is one of the world's toughest critters. Not even a car can squish it.

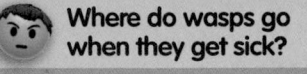

Where do wasps go when they get sick?

The waspital!

23

Spiky spines are another kind of armor. The saddleback caterpillar is armed with spines and horns.

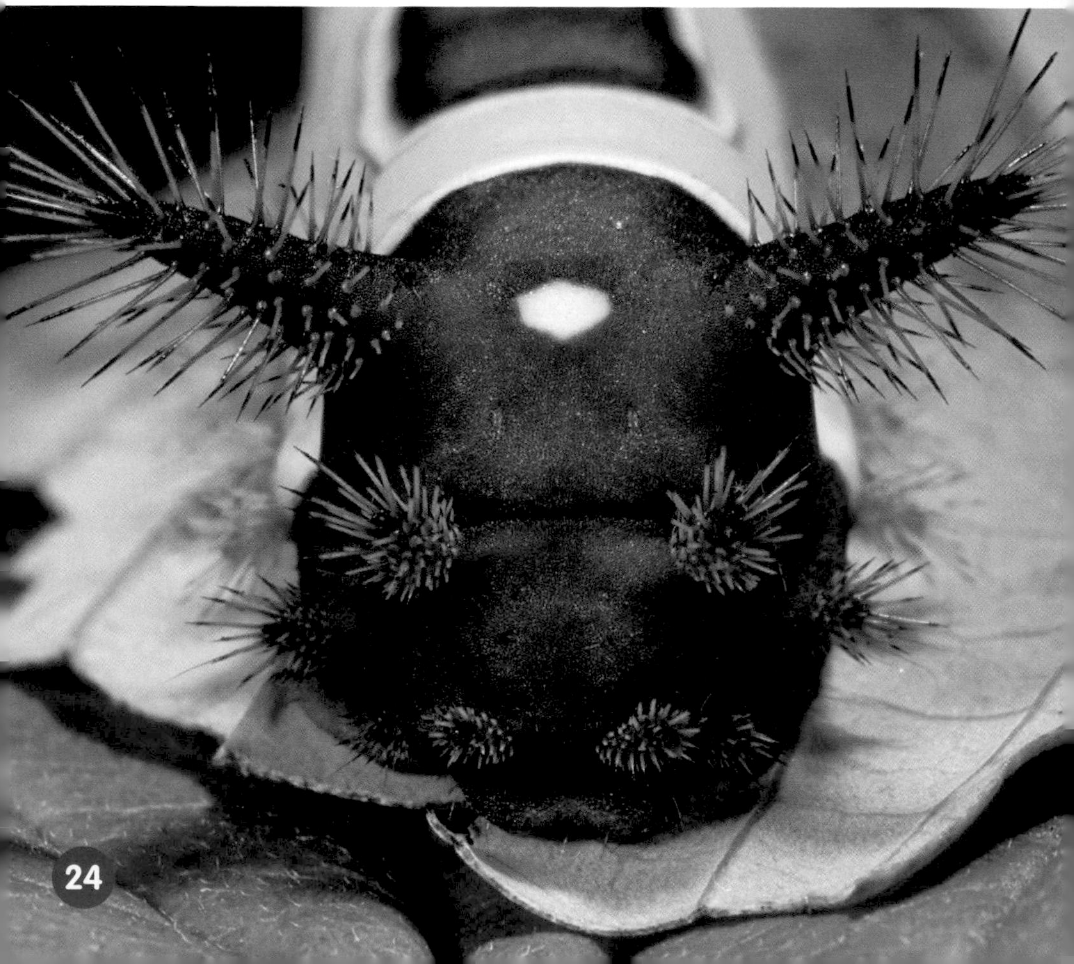

Don't touch! Like Rhino's horns, this caterpillar's sting packs a punch. Its venom can cause swelling and pain.

Camouflage

Miles Morales can escape bad guys by turning invisible so they can't see him. Stick bugs have a different way of turning invisible. They use camouflage to look like twigs!

WEBBY Words

CAMOUFLAGE: An animal's natural color or shape that helps it hide from an enemy

Stick bugs
have an extra
super-power.
If they lose a leg
while escaping an
enemy, they can
grow it back!

THEY HAVE A
LEG UP ON THE
BAD GUYS.

Web-Slinger

Meet the Darwin's bark spider. The web of this itsy-bitsy spider is twice as strong as the web of other spiders. Spider-Man uses his web to catch bad guys. The Darwin's bark spider uses its long web to catch yummy flies.

THWIP

SPIDER-MAN LEARNED A LOT ABOUT BUGS AND THEIR SUPER-POWERS. NOW IT'S TIME TO DISCOVER THE AMAZING BUGS NEAR YOU!

What in the World?

These pictures are close-up views of bugs. Use the hints to help figure out what's in the pictures. Answers are on page 31.

1

HINT: Bees like to hang out here.

2

HINT: This foamy home is protection.

Word Bank

spider legs   dragonfly   spines   mandibles
beehive   froghopper foam

3

HINT: Ouch! These can sting!

4

HINT: These are used to jump far.

5

HINT: These are used to bite things.

6

HINT: It's a fast flier.

GLOSSARY

CAMOUFLAGE: AN ANIMAL'S NATURAL COLOR OR SHAPE THAT HELPS IT HIDE FROM AN ENEMY

HERBIVORE: AN ANIMAL THAT EATS PLANTS

PREDATOR: AN ANIMAL THAT HUNTS AND EATS OTHER ANIMALS

PREY: AN ANIMAL THAT IS EATEN BY ANOTHER ANIMAL